Dash Cryptocurrenc y

Why Dash Digital Currency is the Cryptocurrency of the Future and How You Can Profit from It

Table of Contents

Introduction

I want to thank you and congratulate you for choosing this book, *"Dash Cryptocurrency: Why Dash Digital Currency is the cryptocurrency of the future and how you can profit from it,"* and I sincerely hope you find it useful.

Cryptocurrencies are all the rage right now, and for good reason. They use a revolutionary technology and offer things regular currencies just cannot. There is a good reason for people to get excited about cryptocurrencies and invest in them.

So if you're interested, we're going to take a look at cryptocurrency in detail in this book. You're going to read about the origin of cryptocurrency, important concepts related to it, trading in it and much more. More importantly, we're going to look at one of the most amazing cryptocurrencies available today, Dash.

If you don't know it yet, let me just inform you that Dash is a potent cryptocurrency that solves many of the challenges faced by Bitcoin. We're going to look at its advantages, how you can make money with it, and why it's the hottest cryptocurrency to invest in right now.

So let's get started!

Chapter One: Introduction and History of Cryptocurrency

Cryptocurrency, also known as crypto assets or crypto currency, refers to a medium of exchange which can be efficiently increased by means of secure transactions. Cryptocurrency is an alternate form of currency, a digital currency, the most popular example of which is Bitcoin.

Bitcoin was the first one to bring truly decentralized cryptocurrency into existence in 2009. After that, so many cryptocurrencies have come into existence, like altcoins, which is a merger of Bitcoin's alternatives.

As already mentioned, cryptocurrency is decentralized which further means that it is similar to the Blockchain utilized by the transaction database of Bitcoin as long as a distributed ledger is being used. Furthermore, you can also say that cryptocurrency doesn't operate like the normal system of banking that is highly centralized.

Wei Dai, in 1988, first published an anonymous system of electronic cash, which was known as "b-money." After some time, Nick Szabo created "Bit Gold." Just like Bitcoin, Bit Gold also required users to find solutions to the work functions that are then compiled together and published. After that, Hal Finney, who took inspiration from Wai and Szabo's work, created a currency system. The basis of the system created by Hal Finney was reusable proof of work.

Nakamoto was responsible for the creation of Bitcoin that used a cryptographic hash function known as SHA-256, which further allowed Bitcoin to work as a proof of work system. On the other hand, to decentralize DNS, another system was created in 2011 known as the Name coin. This would make it extremely hard to censor the Internet and not too long after, another currency – Litecoin - was released. Scrypt as a hash function was used for the very first time in this type of cryptocurrency. After that, Peercoin was created which was a hybrid. Peercoin used both the proof of work and proof of stake.

Although various cryptocurrency programs have been created, very few of them have actually been able to integrate into the mainstream economy. Besides, cryptocurrency programs such as Ethereum, NXT as well as Monero marked the second generation of the digital form of currency and were presented to the public in 2014. Some advanced functions like side chains, stealth addresses and smart contracts have been included in these programs.

The credit price of financial institutions is being threatened by cryptocurrencies, which is very similar to blockchain. In addition to the above, increase in the use of cryptocurrencies will eventually lead the consumer to lose their trust confidence in fiat currencies because of the rise in trade with these cryptocurrencies. This will inevitably make it more difficult for the financial institutions to collect data that they need regarding the economic activity which helps the government to steer the economy in the right direction.

A senior banking officer once stated that the increasing utilization of cryptocurrency makes it much more problematic for the statistical agencies to collect the economic data that they need.

The founder of Robocoin, Jordan Kelley, was responsible for the launching of the very first Bitcoin ATM on February 20, 2014. This ATM can be found in Austin, Texas and is very similar to a normal bank ATM. Using the Bitcoin ATM is very similar to using a normal banking ATM, except for the fact that the former allows the user to access any cryptocurrency that they have in their account.

Is it really a currency?

The answer to this question would be yes; cryptocurrency is an exchange medium that uses cryptography to engage in secure transactions and to exercise control over the manufacturing of additional units of the currency. Cryptocurrencies are a type of alternate currency.

Due to the dynamic nature of cryptocurrency, that is recurrent and great changes in its value, one out of the two essentials of money – "a store of value" is missing. Few of the cryptocurrencies display the behavior of fiat currencies that are influenced by inflation where their value is not retained.

History of Cryptocurrency

Although the legal solicitation of cryptocurrencies is documented from the past 7 years, its technical aspects can be traced back to the 1980s, about 30 years ago. David Chaum, a cryptographer, was the first one to theorize the concept of cryptocurrency when he developed an encrypted computer algorithm that allowed unalterable and secure exchange between two parties.

Chaum later founded DigiCash. DigiCash was among the very first companies to produce currency units based on computer algorithms. Contrasting to Bitcoin and other cryptocurrencies where any user is able to mine the currency units (providing they have the necessary skills of computing), only DigiCash Company could produce the currency. The company declared bankruptcy in the late 1990s after they ran into legal problems and rejected a partnership with one of the world's biggest companies, Microsoft, which would have seen DigiCash be a part of every home Windows operating system.

The basis of the architecture behind the cryptocurrencies that we see today can be traced to a white paper published by Wei Dai, a Chinese software engineer, on "b-money." The paper consisted of sensitive information related to complex algorithms, decentralization and anonymity for purchases.

In the 1990s, another failed attempt to create cryptocurrency named E-Gold happened in the US. In exchange of trinkets, coins and jewelry, this company based out of Florida offered tokens of e-gold to their customers. US dollars were traded for these tokens. Initially, the website became successful and more than a million accounts were active on the website in the 2000s. A groundbreaking strategy followed by E-Gold was that anyone was able to open an account on its website. Due to this strategy, a number of scams came to light. Moreover, hacking accidents became prevalent due to poor security protocols, which led to the company going out of business in 2009.

Bitcoin is one of the modern cryptocurrencies, which was first defined by an anonymous entity (the identity of the person or group has never been confirmed) is Satoshi Nakamoto. In early 2009, Bitcoin was released to the public and enthusiasts in large groups started mining, investing and exchanging Bitcoin. In February 2010, the very first Bitcoin market was established.

The first major retailer that supported payment in Bitcoin in late 2012 was WordPress, which is a hosting and website development platform. This allowed Bitcoin to have real-world credibility, which led to large companies showing confidence in Bitcoin.

Download Your FREE BONUS: Cryptocurrency Secrets

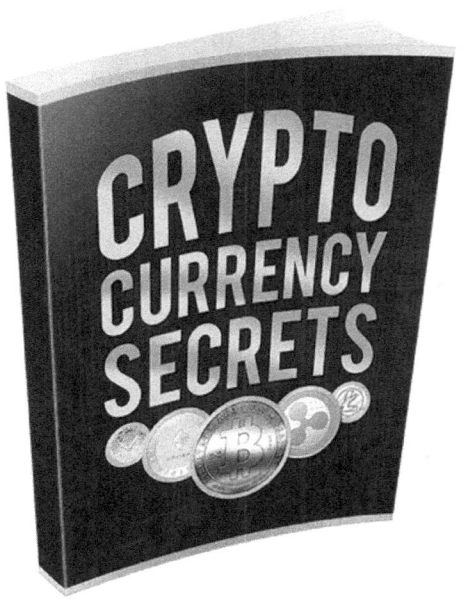

Chapter Two: Important Concepts

Cryptocurrency is a fairly complex system, and to understand it fully, we need to understand some important concepts first. Let's take a look at these concepts in this chapter.

Blockchain

This is something you'll hear about all the time when you discuss a cryptocurrency. That's because the Blockchain is one of the most integral parts of any cryptocurrency. It is basically a list of transactions that keeps growing with each day. Transactions that take place on Bitcoin, Ethereum, and other platforms are linked to specific blocks on the Blockchain, and every such block holds information in a hash pointer that helps it stay connected to the previous block in the chain. Whenever a transaction takes place and is accepted into the chain, a time stamp is attached to it so the users can check when the deal took place.

In the early '90s, Stuart Haber and W. Scott Stornetta studied Merkle trees to find more efficient ways of collecting data from blocks. This was the first work involving secure Blockchains. The Satoshi Nakamoto group conceptualized the first distribution of Blockchain in 2008 when they were working on Bitcoin public ledger's core components.

The Bitcoin Blockchain is based on a peer-to-peer network. The transaction gets sealed after having a time stamp placed on it and the Blockchain is distributed through a server. The database is autonomously managed so there can be no double spending unless an administrator says that's alright.

Fun fact: the Bitcoin Blockchain was 20 GB in 2014 and at the time of writing this, it is over 140 GB in size. Actually, wait, that's probably not really fun. It is, in fact, one of the biggest problems of the Bitcoin that is going to hamper its scalability.

Blockchain 2.0 was introduced later to help the users write smart contracts in a refined manner. The technology goes beyond just transactions. An off-chain oracle protocol was implemented in 2016 in which the oracle gets access to data that is not on the network. It also helps in predicting the market conditions.

Some blocks don't get chosen to be included in the Blockchain, and they are called orphan blocks. Since there are multiple supported versions of blocks, only one can survive in the end, and the one surviving is the highest scoring one. No block is guaranteed, but the blocks can't write over each other at any point causing the placement of duplicate data on the Blockchain.

Smart Contract

Contracts made with computer code and which operate on the Blockchain are what we call smart contracts. They verify and enforce contracts on their own, making our jobs much easier, and they seldom require external operators since they're usually self-executing. Many industries use this technology as anything of value can be exchanged through these smart contracts.

Since smart contracts run on a decentralized network, they remove the risk of fraud, non-compliance with the terms of contract, unauthorized changes and other things. They operate automatically, executing when the terms of the contract are met and withholding when they're not. Any changes made to contracts can also be tracked since every version will be stored on the Blockchain with a timestamp on it. It gives a much more accurate picture of the whole process. Since the ledger can't be tampered with, there is no need for third-party intermediation and everyone is more honest because of them.

Decentralized Applications

Decentralized Applications, or DApps, are what we call open source applications, which are not controlled by a single person or entity. They are run on a network of computers connected to each other via peer-to-peer connections and there is no central server.

Since decentralized apps run on a network of computers and the users decide all the changes, they are not prone to downtime, server crashes and hacking. This is because for all these things to happen, there needs to be a central point that *can* be crashed or hacked. Since there are thousands of computers on the network, one or few of them going offline won't affect the app and it keeps running smoothly at all times. One single hacked computer also cannot make any unapproved changes to the application, as any change that happens needs to be agreed to by the majority of the network.

Working

The Blockchain never keeps your data in one place all the time. Ad hoc messages are used on the distributed network because the Blockchain lacks a centralized server. It lacks the vulnerable points that can be exploited by hackers in a centralized system. Methods like public key cryptography are used to enhance Blockchain's security. So if someone wants to send you coins, they will need your public key, which is just a string of random letters and numbers to identify you. For private keys, passwords are needed for accessing your assets. It is recommended to keep both your password *and* your private key to yourself since it is very critical to your account's security.

You can understand the concept of public and private keys in another way. Think of them as your phone number and your phone's passcode respectively. Anyone having your phone number can contact you and send you information, which is how a public key works. On the other hand, only you should have access to what's inside your phone. This is protected by a passcode in the same way your account is protected by a private key.

There is no central authority responsible for controlling the system, so nobody can manipulate information on the network. Any decentralized system eventually reaches a point where nothing can be hidden from the users and everyone on the network can see whatever is on the network.

Every node on the Blockchain network has a copy of the Blockchain on it, and there is no centralized copy that exists. This means that no user is trusted more than the others. Every transaction that happens on the network will be broadcast on the network so everyone can see it. Mining nodes work on validating transactions. They create blocks before and then broadcast to other nodes from those blocks to verify the operations. Timestamp schemes are also used to keep the system serialized and organized.

As the data keeps getting bigger, the nodes will have to keep growing in computational power because of the sheer amount of computer resources required to process that data. This means that things will get more expensive and the risk of node centralization will increase. This is one risk that will always be present in the technology until a different system is developed.

Download Your FREE BONUS: Cryptocurrency Secrets

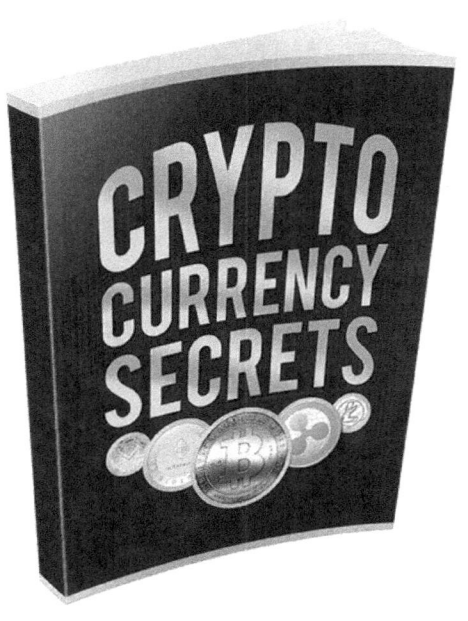

Chapter Three: Trading and Investing in Cryptocurrency

This chapter is going to be all about how to trade and invest in cryptocurrencies, but before we do that, we need to learn how to acquire them and store them. Since pretty much all cryptocurrencies are stored and traded in the same way, I'm going to illustrate the process by taking the example of Bitcoin.

In order to invest and trade in cryptocurrencies, you have to first learn how to store them and buy them. Almost all cryptocurrencies are stored, bought and traded in the same manner, so we are going to take the example of Bitcoin to understand what the process is.

Acquiring

While not the cheapest or even the easiest, computer mining seems to be the most popular way of acquiring Bitcoins so far. Mining is a practice of solving complex mathematical equations on computers that results in the miner earning some free Bitcoins for their work. This is how the very first Bitcoins were created and how more of them keep entering the system.

Another way of acquiring Bitcoins, a much easier one, is to simply find a Bitcoin exchange and buy some Bitcoins. There are multiple exchanges that exist for Bitcoin trading, some better than others. Take your time researching a few popular ones and pick wisely so you won't be scammed. Avoid anything that sounds too good to be true.

Always make sure you research the exchange well, so you eliminate the risk of getting ripped off. Individuals who claim to help you mine Bitcoins are not to be believed and will try to scam you in most cases. Any cryptocurrency that has a high-value today will attract parties with malicious intent. Be smart and don't fall victim to their trickery. Another thing that you should steer clear of is pyramid-schemes involving Bitcoin. People can make them sound very profitable on paper, but in reality, they don't really pan out and can rip off all your funds permanently.

Understand that even with all the scams floating around, cryptocurrencies are still worth investing in. Just like traditional currencies still hold value despite the scams surrounding them, so do cryptocurrencies. Sure, they may not be as essential to our daily lives as conventional fiat currencies, but can still be highly valuable to you if you know how to invest intelligently. Just make sure you buy from trustworthy sources and do your research. Identify a good exchange and then you're free to start trading to your heart's desire. Avoiding scams in the cryptocurrency world isn't hard. You just need to make smart, logical decisions.

Storing

Just like traditional currency requires a wallet for safekeeping, so does cryptocurrency. When you buy Bitcoin, a digital wallet is automatically created for you, which holds your Bitcoins from that point forward. Anytime you buy or spend your Bitcoins, your wallet will be updated to show the current state.

The wallet exists on your personal computer as well as cloud storage, and operates just like a bank, except in this case; you are your own bank. You can use your wallet for a number of purposes like sending or receiving money, paying for goods and much more.

You should understand, however, that digital wallets are not risk-free and some things may cause irreversible damage to your funds. The FDIC doesn't insure the wallet; so don't expect your insurance company's help in case of any loss of money in case of discrepancies in your wallet. Where you choose to store your wallet is also important. A digital wallet stored in the cloud may be subject to the whims of the storage company. Not only that, you could lose all your money if their servers get hacked. The same thing can happen if you store your wallet on your own computer. Your computer can be hacked or infected with viruses. And if it ever fails completely, you may lose everything in your wallet permanently.

Trading

As we step into 2018, NASDAQ will start trading Bitcoin futures, thus marking an important chapter in the history of cryptocurrency. Cryptocurrencies have been extremely volatile these past few years, seeing violent swings in value just in a single day. This prompts people to buy and sell several times in 24 hours, sometimes even hundreds of times. With the official launch of Bitcoin on NASDAQ, trading will become even more lucrative who held fast during the tough times.

To start trading, you should first decide on which cryptocurrencies you want to trade in. Some people use only one, making big profits or losses on just that. Others like to diversify and capitalize on market trends in the whole crypto-economy. Once you've settled on the cryptocurrencies you will be using, the next thing to do is to find a suitable trading platform and decide your strategies. Start by learning the ways of the market, working under an experienced trader. It's a very effective technique.

Making money

Let's take a look at some ways to make money with cryptocurrencies in this section.

Accept cryptocurrencies as payment

If you run a business of any sort, you can request your customers to pay you in cryptocurrencies. It doesn't matter whether you have a physical store or just an online business, you can receive cryptocurrency payments with the help of specific apps that enable you to do so. The list of payment methods available today is nearly inexhaustible, so you may find customers that are willing to buy exclusively from you simply because you let them pay you in whatever way they want to. If your friends and family owe you any money, you can also ask them to send it to you in cryptocurrency. All you need to do is give them your account address.

Mine cryptocurrencies

Mining refers to the process of creating new tokens of a cryptocurrency by solving a puzzle of complex mathematical equations through computers. This is done to verify the transactions placed into a block. Miners who use their computers to solve these equations are given some new tokens as a reward.

Before you start mining, however, you need to carefully analyze your options and decide which one you want to mine. The Bitcoin market is so saturated right now that it is no longer profitable to mine Bitcoins. Mining requires powerful computers and a lot of energy, so you need a cheap source of energy to remain profitable. For cryptocurrencies like Dash and LSK, you need special permissions/privileges to mine, so keep that in mind.

Alternatively, you can also join a mining pool and then earn rewards based on how much computation power you contributed. This is a way for people who don't have very powerful computers to mine cryptocurrencies.

Create your own cryptocurrencies

You might be skeptical about this one, but it's a legit way of making money, albeit a tad radical. There are some websites, like Counterparty, which let you create your own cryptocurrency on the site's blockchain.

Great! That seems easy, let's do it.

But hold your horses. Why would anyone want to invest in your cryptocurrency? Most new cryptocurrencies come and go every day without gaining any significant value. You have to remember that money, or anything really, holds value because people demand it. If there's no demand, the item has no value. Take the case of Bitcoin. It took years of people believing in its premise for it to gain any actual market value. First came the social capital and demand, then came the monetary value.

So you must understand by now that merely creating a cryptocurrency won't give you any profits. In fact, you will most probably suffer losses, as you won't even be able to cover your initial capital expenditure. What you need to do is figure out a way to make people want your cryptocurrency. Come up with a marketable idea and then build a dApp on Ethereum, Lisk, or something similar. There are many existing apps like that already, like Augur and FirstBlood. Both these apps fulfill the needs of a particular market, and that's why people use them. So the best way to make money from your own cryptocurrency is by tying it to a marketable business idea and then building a dApp around it.

Keep in mind that this method is not for everyone. Not all of us have the resources, intelligence, skills, or the mental fortitude to pull this off.

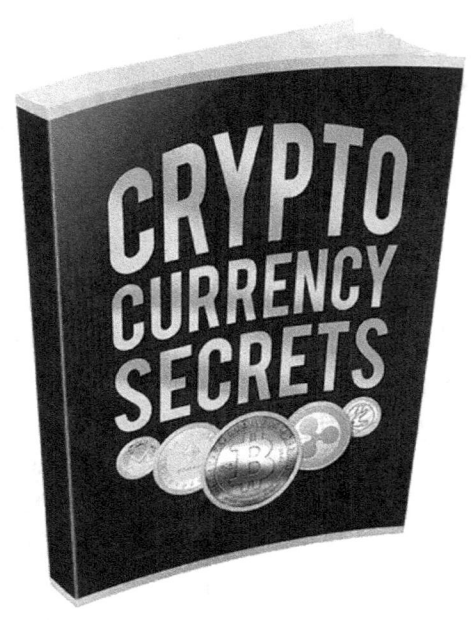

Chapter Four: Challenges of Bitcoin

In the last seven or so years of its existence, Bitcoin has come a very long way but still, there's so much apprehension amongst people to use it as the recognized method for the payment of goods and services. Following are several challenges faced by Bitcoin to be seen as a mainstream method for the purpose of payment and what is likely to happen if the consumers begin to use digital currency on a large scale.

1. Volatility

Since its inception, Bitcoin has been considered extremely volatile. The Bitcoin that was worth $10 in 2010 is now worth millions of dollars in 2017. And this is not at all slowing down – in fact, it is increasing by the second.

Amongst speculators, Bitcoin has become very popular. They buy Bitcoin in the hope that its price will rise continuously. This doesn't help Bitcoin to gain popularity as a currency to be used widely for the payment of goods and services. For instance, if you plan to take a vacation and keep aside $1000 for the same by storing it in Bitcoin, its purchasing power could fall or climb significantly by the time you'll actually leave. Usually, most people are averse to that kind of risk. Its price needs to gain more stability for it to gain mainstream acceptance.

2. Ease of use

Although over the years, it has become much easier and convenient to buy, sell and use Bitcoin, still it hasn't gained the user-friendly quality to be chosen as a mainstream currency. At the present time, if a normal person has the desire to buy a Bitcoin, he/she will first need to open an account at a Bitcoin exchange like Coinbase, then would have to link a checking account or his/her credit card (which comes with higher fees) and in most cases, would have to wait for several days for the transaction to get cleared.

With the entrance of Square (NYSE:SQ) and companies similar to it, the potential for Bitcoin to fix these issues has risen. In other words, if there's a mobile application that is used by people anyway, like Square Cash, that would allow people to purchase Bitcoin with just a touch of their fingers, it would become very easy for less tech-savvy users to adapt to digital currencies.

3. Widespread acceptance

Consumers can pay for Bitcoin transactions with the help of several online retailers; however, digital currency is a long shot away from getting acceptance all over the world. If Square, or any other payment processing corporate, chooses to allow retailers who are using their hardware to accept payments in Bitcoin easily, it can easily turn around the entire game for adopting Bitcoin in the mainstream market.

4. Potential for theft

Although there are security measures which makes it impossible to virtually steal Bitcoins, but to gain benefit from them, the user needs to have a complex knowledge about its working. True enthusiasts of Bitcoin would not mind taking more efforts, but the ease of use challenge faced by Bitcoins discussed earlier holds its ground. Also, whenever you're using Bitcoin wallets online, there's always a slight chance that your currency might get stolen. It has taken place before and it can certainly happen again.

5. Reputation for criminal activity

In its early days, Bitcoin was majorly known for its usage on Dark Web, to buy illegal items or to engage in money-laundering activities. It makes sense also. Bitcoin is the only anonymous source of payment in the real world, so it became an obvious choice for people who wanted to purchase illegal weapons, drugs, etc. Also, because of its anonymous source of payment, it will be very difficult to have a solution for this problem, if not impossible.

The anonymous nature of Bitcoin can be one of its positive aspects, but its illicit use is always a threat.

6. Tax issues

The Bitcoin and other digital currencies are considered to be "intangible property" by the IRS under the current law, which means that these currencies are subject to capital gains taxes.

Every time a Bitcoin is bought and sold for more than what was paid for it, the difference on tax needs to be reported. From the perspective of a currency, it is much worse. Anytime a Bitcoin is used to purchase something, it potentially becomes a taxable event. For instance, if for a cup of coffee, originally priced at $4, is bought by some customer at $5 in Bitcoin, then the difference in both the prices is technically a capital gain. Well, this situation will create the need for exhaustive recordkeeping and the users of Bitcoin are left with the following three choices: Maintain detailed records of every transaction done through Bitcoin, take the risk to get into trouble with the IRS or not use Bitcoin ever.

To be rational, profits coming out of any currency can lead to a taxable income, but it generally does not happen on a routine basis. After all, there are very few people in the US who regularly make payment in euros or yen.

7. Scalability

If technical details are somewhat overseen, Bitcoin has a serious problem of scalability. The blockchain, which is the fundamental technology behind Bitcoin, has put a limit on the amount of information that each block can contain. Only 1 megabyte of data can be contained in each of the blocks. The maximum network capacity is, thus, three transactions per second because of this limitation.

This means that as trade through Bitcoin is increased, it will get more difficult for the network to keep up, which can further result in grave processing delays. For instance, the average network capacity of Visa is 2,000 transactions per second, which is way higher than Bitcoin. Therefore, if Bitcoin wants to get into mainstream adoption, it will have to fix this issue. Despite so many solutions already put on the table, a long-term solution is still awaited.

[Download Your FREE BONUS: Cryptocurrency Secrets](#)

Chapter Five: Dash Digital Cash

Dash; previously called XCoin and Darkcoin, works as a peer-to-peer open source cryptocurrency. On top of acquiring the feature set of Bitcoin, it presently offers the chance of private trades (PrivateSend), instant trades (InstantSend) and operates on a self-funding and self-governing model that allows the Dash network to make payment to businesses and individuals for performing tasks and activities that help in adding value to the network. The budgeting system and decentralized governance of Dash allow it to become a decentralized autonomous organization (DAO).

History

Evan Duffield released Dash on January 18th, 2014. The Dash cryptocurrency allows transaction between two users without the involvement of any third party. The Dash digital cash was introduced after Bitcoin and its valued determination is now possible in the market. All across the world, Dash has a huge value of exchange and it is independent of any central authority for engaging in any financial transaction.

Dash relaunch

The name of the cryptocurrency changed to "Darkcoin" on February 28th, 2014. Almost a year later, Darkcoin was renamed as "Dash" on March 25th, 2015. To this date, more than 1.9 million coins have been mined which contribute to around a quarter of the present supply of Dash. The developer of Dash, Evan Duffield, credited "instamine" to code error that further increased the problem rather than solving it. After that, Duffield wanted to relaunch Dash minus instamine, but there was disapproval coming from the cryptocurrency community. Thereafter, to escalate the distribution of coins, coins he suggested "airdrop." Although the initial distribution of coins was left in the middle, development of the project continued.

Core team of Dash

At the time of launch of Dash, cryptocurrency was considered to be a term synonymous with scams. Dash was one of the very few survivors of scams. The core team of Dash did the development of digital currency. The core team has now expanded to 50 employees, out of which 20 employees work part-time and 30 of them are full-time employees and in addition to them, there are plenty of volunteers. The payments were made to these employees through Dash's budget system. To avoid conflict of interest, they never rely on donations or sponsorships. Up until now, Dash has been able to resolve many issues like slow time of confirmation, increased size of block, decentralized governance and self-funding development budget.

Features

Following are the major features of Dash Digital Cash:

Masternodes

Dash uses a two-tier network, which is contrary to Bitcoin that uses a single-tier network, where miners on the network perform each and every job. Miners handle certain functions of the network, like creating new blocks. Dash network's second tier includes "Masternodes" which are responsible for performing InstantSend, PrivateSend and governance functions.

In order to prevent Sybil attacks, masternodes need Collateral, which is equal to 1000 Dash. This can be spent any time. Although, using these collaterals will remove the network from the associated network. Since significant network functions are performed by masternodes, there is a split in the block rewards between masternodes and miners, with each of the group earning 45% of the reward. Remaining 10% of the block reward is responsible for funding the "treasury" or "budget" system.

PrivateSend

PrivateSend, based on CoinJoin, is a coin mixing service, with various modifications. PrivateSend includes utilizing masternodes as an alternative to a single website, connecting by blending multiple masternodes, limiting the mixing to accept certain denominations only and passive node. 1000 Dash is the maximum limit for a PrivateSend transaction.

In reiterations at the later stages, advanced methods were used for pre-mixing denominations that were built into the cryptocurrency wallet of the user. Implementing PrivateSend allowed the masternodes to submit transactions through DSTX, which is a special network code. Unlike other CoinJoin based implementations like CoinShuffle and DarkWallet, DSTX provided additional security to users by tackling the dead change issue found in CoinShuffle and DarkWallet.

DarkSend was rebranded as PrivateSend in June 2016.

In its present implementation, PrivateSend adds privacy to all the transactions by joining multiple users to identical inputs to initiate a single transaction using various outputs. Since the funds are identical, it is not possible to directly trace the transactions, thus, obscuring the fund flow. PrivateSend made dash "fungible." Mixing the coins of similar value with other wallets, made sure that the value of all coins remained the same☐

InstantSend

To allow almost immediate transactions, InstantSend service can be used. With the help of this system, the consensus of the masternode network can be used to lock a particular transaction and verify it. Those blocks and transactions are rejected which seems to be conflicting. If it is not possible to reach a consensus, standard block confirmation can be used to validate the transactions. The problem of double spending can be solved by InstantSend without having to wait for a longer time of confirmation as in the case of other cryptocurrencies like Bitcoin.

InstantX was rebranded as InstantSend in June 2016.

Dash market cap

In June 2017, as per the Coin Market Cap, the market capitalization of Dash was over $1.4 billion and the volume of trade was approximately $100 Million per day. Dash became one of the most active altcoin community, having 133k replies, 7.9 million reads and above 6400 pages. In order to increase the network power, Dash uses a two-tier architecture. The first tier belongs to miners that simultaneously engage in transactions and provide security to the network. The second-tier belongs to masternodes that enable the advanced features of Dash.

Future prospects

As time passed, people realized the significance of Dash in solving real-world problems of digital currency. Now, users have started investing in cryptocurrencies and in not too long, Dash's market capitalization will be highest in comparison to other cryptocurrencies. In the very first year, Dash was able to overcome many of the technical hurdles and it is one of the most sought-after digital currencies in the market.

Download Your FREE BONUS: Cryptocurrency Secrets

Chapter Six: Advantages of Dash Digital Cash
Low expense

Unlike Banks or Visas, Dash expenses are much lower. Even when there are no expenses regularly, no one charges you a ton of money to utilize your own funds and installments of miniaturized scale can be sent anytime and anywhere on the planet.

Instant payments

A lot of opportunities are set aside to sustain exchanges on Bitcoin and other advanced monetary standards, thus being quick with respect to exchanges done through banks. Usually, traders need 5-6 affirmations to consider the exchanged as finished. In Bitcoin, normally it takes 10 minutes to affirm a single exchange.

A 50-60 hour elongated time for exchange might give satisfaction so as to make installments on the web (where it is okay to not send the merchandise for a long time), this renders almost every computerized cash irrational for things like in-store or up close and personal purchasing and can restrain its potential.

Dash engineers have made a cutting-edge, decentralized innovation known as InstantX. InstantX can certify and affirm installments in approximately four seconds. It might be hard to believe, but it's true that in a couple of moments you can transfer cash anywhere.

Expanded privacy

In the world of digital currency, an open record is maintained where anyone is able to check the exchanges as they happen. Also, it is vital to have a general society record – the conviction each individual shows in the framework takes its origin from the manner in which everybody on the system can act as a reviewer to approve that the working of the framework is accurate.

In advanced forms of money such as Bitcoin, "open keys" or "locations" are used by individuals in sending and getting cash. These locations consist of a series of characters and often look like the following:

XrEgRgW6JkrsY38QGV65rnmKBRZ7KSRktv

A pseudonymous framework, where clients do not use their own name, is used but as time passes by various trades, administrations, sellers and people that clients interact with can join your own information to your address.

Once your address has been related to your character, that significant information can be used for tracking your payments and other exchanges or may be sold to other people or agencies such as culprits, charge specialists, advertisers. You can get connected to the whole of your exchange history in an event of sending cash to an individual or a substance.

A major right foreseen by Dash is budgetary protection. Consequently, Dash allowed the clients to exchange with sincere protection, so no one could connect a specific exchange or address to the character of a man. By using Dash, it is possible for the clients to keep their exchanges secure and private.

Two-tier network

The foremost cryptocurrency to display the "masternodes" idea is Dash. These are servers which in association with Dash are "dependable, secure and furnished for conveying several organizations in the system itself. Now, these servers are used to strengthen the moment exchanges and protection highlights

At the later stages, they can be used to familiarize the system with a new administration that other digital currencies can't do. There's an additional guarantee given by this two-tier system. It equips Dash with a cutting-edge, robust framework, which provides its clients an abnormal state of administration.

Well defined governance model

Administration of a crypto-cash venture is essentially vital for everyone, even for people who may have certain prejudices. For example, despite being the most predominant and well-financed digital currency, Bitcoin is completely dependent on deliberate commitments from private foundations and institutions.

It has rendered Bitcoin feeble and powerless against the instincts of these private organizations. Because of sincere difference amongst the engineers of Bitcoin regarding specific parts of Bitcoin's answer does not give away a characterized way of determinations, thus, provoking worry in media over where the task is heading and the capability to defeat the question.

Amusingly, to enhance Dash, receive endorsement and store these propositions directly from the income of the system, it has a characterized set of instruments for anyone to give recommendations directly to the system. For end-clients, it becomes critical for various reasons. To begin with, there comes a guarantee with it that Dash is devoid of the effects of key promoters and can focus on communicating its central mission to its clients.

Secondly, any disagreements regarding the potential advancement of the innovation can be determined through this, which ensures coherence in the administration of the system. Next, it solidifies every worthy enhancement or venture so that they have a chance to be subsidized, notwithstanding the prospect that the benefits are spread over the whole system. It can be trusted that the administration instruments of Dash will benefit its clients at last by conveying the principal arrangement.

Sharing

Not so long ago, every exchange of asset done by you was absolutely subjected to banks. Banks are capable of impeding your record, debase or they can even appropriate your cash. Currently, there's a decision that needs to be made – with Dash, you can control each of your assets by your own wallet and exchanges done through cash can also be confirmed and controlled by a conveyed arrangement. The need for delegates and their charges is disposed of by the decentralized system of the clients present worldwide.

Security

Dash is a type of digital money certified by using driven cryptography. These changes are organized by the energy transferred by numerous free computer systems present everywhere in the world, rather than getting these exchanges prepared through banks. Dash functions on a decentralized system are secured, and its power is its two-tier engineering system. The source code of Dash is open and is accessible to everyone to see and verify it. This guarantees the wellbeing, security, and autonomy of the framework. A Two-tier structure and propelled encryption are used by Dash organize to secure the assets of the clients.

Worldwide infrastructure and payments

Cash exchange can happen anyplace with anyone with a Dash wallet. Outsiders will not be able to follow or hinder these exchanges.

Less demanding international trade

Digital Currency standards comprehend several wasteful aspects in the budgetary framework, for instance, provoking cash exchanges globally and electronic installments for a small amount of money. The digital currency standards are uniting people in a world that is closing down the gaps and is considering a worldwide collaboration, which is free of neighborhood cash or a man's area

Since expenses are meager or non-existent, it strengthens the trade of installments that are small scale for the purpose of administration that have neither reason nor rhyme to utilize the higher cost cash exchange structures.

Latest business opportunities

In today's world, monitory standards that are advanced in nature like Dash are exposed to a different universe of business opportunities altogether, thus, making it vital to get comfortable with this innovation.

With the rise of web and innovations relating to systems administration, the enhancement of these digital currencies paves a way for several opportunities in the form of providing administration and foundation directly recognized with Dash, or to have a level of comfort with the manner in which it works and propose it as an esteem alternative, as in the case of any customary business, to its clients.

In the development of digital currency, Dash has particularly been a pioneer. It has been the first to operate in momentary exchanges, security highlights, and several other imaginative highlights. It has become essential to get accustomed with innovations happening globally, hold some amount of digital currency, figure out the importance of using a wallet to receive and send cash and without any exertion, new thoughts will automatically start coming up regarding the application of this vigorous innovation in your daily routine.

Early adopter advantage: Investment potential

The future of Dash looks extremely encouraging and the highlights given by Dash organization seem to be extremely valuable for individuals all across the globe. If you are an early adopter of the Dash digital cash, the likelihood of your Dash currency to rise and develop as an incentive after some time is tremendous. Obviously, there is a threat of changes in the value, yet Dash has definitely turned out to be a stable one in contrast with other forms of cryptocurrency.

Download Your FREE BONUS: Cryptocurrency Secrets

Chapter Seven: The cryptocurrency investor's mindset

Your mindset is the most important factor when it comes to doing anything in life, and unsurprisingly, this applies to investing as well. No amount of theory can help you invest well if you don't have the right mindset. So here are some of the mindset attributes a successful cryptocurrency investor has.

Think long-term

Any significant investment on your part should be a long-term endeavor. This is true for any type of investment, not just cryptocurrency. So think of it as a marathon, not a sprint. You don't reach your dream destinations by taking a quick, breezy walk. And if you try to cover a long journey by sprinting, you will probably burn out before you're anywhere close to your destination. So think long-term when investing in cryptocurrencies.

Genuine positivity

Positivity is a great thing to have because we all know that negativity doesn't help you accomplish anything. However, there is a difference between genuine positivity and forced positivity. When you're faced with a tough situation, face the truth and find positives in it realistically. When you suffer a loss, be positive about the lesson you've learned from said loss, not about the loss itself. That would be silly.

Avoid going "all in"

Often, when people start losing some money in a casino, they get anxious about it and start thinking of ways to recover it all back quickly. They try to put all their remaining money on a single bet. While this may seem like a great way of quickly earning back all our money in one go, it can also lead to losing everything. Most people don't consider this, but the better option here is to take a breather and start building up your funds by small, strategic plays. Of course, investing in cryptocurrencies isn't like gambling, but the analogy still stands.

You can't win all the time

No matter how well read and smart you are, you cannot always win. There are bound to be some investments that don't give you the return you expected or any return at all. Newbie investors often make the mistake of thinking they can win all of their investments, but that's very naïve. When you enter this market, make sure you understand beforehand that you can't win every single time and that it takes years to build a good win-loss ratio.

Small profits are good profits

Somebody once told me that when you make a hundred small profits, they eventually turn into one huge profit. To this day, I think that this statement is 100% true. If you keep looking for that one in a million huge profit you may never find, you will just waste your time and resources. Instead, focus on making small profits regularly and that will slowly build up your portfolio. Always have realistic positivity, as we've already discussed.

Learn to cut your losses

Sometimes, things just don't go your way, and all your plans are for naught. This is when you decide to cut your losses and exit. The market isn't anyone's slave and if you don't exit at the right time, you will lose more money 9 out of 10 times. Many people let their pride take over and hold onto their losses thinking they can recover from them eventually. That's almost never true and the investment they hold soon becomes worthless. So always remember the old saying, "Cut your losses and ride your winners!"

Question everything

When it comes to investing, no amount of research is enough research. Never make assumptions about anything and always research what you're going to invest in. The more you question, the more you'll learn, and the more informed decisions you will make.

Questioning yourself and everything around you is the best way to improve yourself. Get into a habit of self-improvement by asking important questions often. Learn what works and what doesn't.

Be patient and persistent

Most people want an instant payday, and since they don't usually get it, they sell out their cryptocurrencies early and miss out on the profits. You need to be patient and wait for your investment to gain value. If you refuse to do that, you're just going to lose money and complain about it later because somebody else who was patient made money that you didn't.

Tyler and Cameron Winklevoss bought Bitcoin worth $11 million in 2013 and today; it is worth over $230 million. Their patience paid off, whereas many people who sold during this period because of market fluctuations and negative press must've suffered losses.

So develop the self-discipline needed to just wait and watch what happens. Don't fidget too much when there are market fluctuations and resist selling when the price falls. This brings me to my next point.

Ignore the media

Warren Buffett has admitted to living in Omaha simply because he wanted to stay away from Wall Street and its "experts". He has often said that he ignores the press and does his own research. The Winklevoss twins also didn't pay attention to the media when investing in Bitcoin and invested a big sum when the Bitcoin was quite unpopular because of negative press coverage. Today, their investment is worth 20 times more.

What I'm trying to say is that paying attention to the media and its "experts" is a recipe for disaster and causes people to lose their money. After the Gox exchange being hacked in 2013, many people dumped their cryptocurrencies and they became synonymous with Ponzi schemes and frauds in the eyes of laypeople. But smart investors who didn't listen to the media and made their own independent choices are now raking in millions.

Have thick skin

Expanding on the previous point, let your own judgment guide you and have thick skin so you can handle criticism when it inevitably comes your way. Believing in yourself and trusting your own judgments is a very liberating feeling, and once you have developed the self-confidence necessary to do this, you will become a much more successful investor. Don't let anyone else do the thinking for you, be it family, friends, or the media experts.

Be a total geek

In its simplest forms, geek means someone who gets excited and obsesses over things most people don't, even the technical details. You could say Warren Buffett is a huge geek when it comes to reading financial reports. In fact, he can spend hours and hours studying corporate earnings, trying to find out who the biggest moneymakers are.

If an investor of his caliber does it, you'd think that more people would understand the importance of it, but they don't. If you want to be successful, you *have* to be a complete geek about it. Devote as much time as you can to study cryptocurrency and learn everything you can about it. Eat, sleep, talk cryptocurrency and really get into the hard numbers! That's how you make a fortune.

Pay attention to market cap

A rookie investor just looks at the price of a cryptocurrency and makes the buying decision, but another thing should influence your decision, and that is the market cap of the cryptocurrency. It is the number you get when you multiply the current price of the cryptocurrency with its current supply, and it matters more than the price, because a cryptocurrency having a higher price may have a lower market cap than one that has a lower price.

Take the example of Bitcoin Cash and Ethereum. While Bitcoin Cash's price is much higher than that of Ethereum right now, the latter has a market cap of almost twice as much as that of the former. This means that Ethereum has a higher future survivability than Bitcoin Cash. Price increases are great in the short term, but you're in this for the long run, so pay more attention to the market capitalization when making the final decision.

Don't diversify just for the sake of it

"Don't put all your eggs in one basket" is a popular saying, and it's especially popular in the investment circle. Many investors like to diversify just for the sake of diversifying, but that's honestly a horrible strategy if you don't know what you're doing. In the cryptocurrency ecosystem, you have so many cryptocurrencies that are not going to survive for long, and investing in them without proper research pretty much guarantees you're going to lose your "eggs".

Don't follow traditional investment advice when it comes to cryptocurrency investment. Diversify only based on certain predetermined parameters, like market capitalization, current price, and utility. If you don't believe there is a good future for the cryptocurrency, you best avoid it.

Don't sell everything when the market is hot

The cryptocurrency phenomenon today is being termed as a bubble simply because now that it has gained some traction, everyone is jumping on the bandwagon to make a quick buck. Most of these investors invest some amount in a cryptocurrency of their choice and when its price increases significantly, they sell it. But you don't want to do that. You want to think long-term and always keep your ultimate goal in mind, which is to constantly increase in value.

So take your time in identifying cryptocurrencies that you think have a long lifespan. These cryptocurrencies, even if they fall today, will rise again. Don't look at things with a short-term eye. Learn to look into the future so you can tell for yourself which cryptocurrencies are worth keeping and which ones deserve to be dumped.

Most of them are going to die

There are over a thousand cryptocurrencies in the world right now and the market is growing steadily with a new one entering every week. It can be difficult to tell which ones are good and which ones aren't. The best and easiest way to do it is by asking yourself this question: "Does this cryptocurrency have anything unique to offer?"

If the answer is yes, the cryptocurrency might survive, otherwise, it's going to die. It may happen in a few months or even a few years, but unless it has something unique to offer, it's definitely not going to survive the brutal market. Cryptocurrencies like Dash, Monero, Bitcoin, Ethereum, and Litecoin all have something great to offer. They solve some problem, and they do it well, so people are going to keep investing in them.

Most other cryptocurrencies have no special purpose. They're just coins that just build upon the original Bitcoin blockchain technology. You must've seen many of these around if you're already a part of the market. They're not worth your time, so you're much better off investing in cryptocurrencies that solve a problem.

Download Your FREE BONUS: Cryptocurrency Secrets

Conclusion

We've reached the end of this book, and to conclude it, I would just like to say that cryptocurrencies are not a fad and they're here to stay. It's a novel system and it will continue to live on in some form or another. As an investor, the best thing you can do is learn how to read the market and make sound decisions for the future. Your ability to analyze, research, make the right choice, and ultimately be willing to face the truth will take you a long way.

I hope you enjoyed reading this book as much as I enjoyed writing it. A variety of topics have been covered, so take your time and read up on them in detail. Take your investment potential to the next level and make money with Dash, the smartest cryptocurrency in the market right now.

Thank you so much for reading this book and all the best!

Resources

https://www.youtube.com/watch?v=du-xvKfGeeU

https://www.youtube.com/watch?v=B6-q-73-phU

https://www.youtube.com/watch?v=vFwXeFk6VO8

https://www.youtube.com/watch?v=r7erSqaRRnw

www.ingramcontent.com/pod-product-compliance
Lightning Source LLC
Chambersburg PA
CBHW071240220526
45468CB00002B/940